WALL STREET

ROULETTE

What the new trader needs to know, simply written to be understood by persons with a tenth grade education. No fancy math or equations, just straight truth as experienced by a diligent trader for six years.

Stan Wilder

DEDICATION

TO MY DAD, WHO NEVER BOUGHT A STOCK

.

CONTENTS

ACKNOWLEDGMENTS

Investopedia.com for the many descriptions and terms I've researched there..

CHAPTER 1
WALL STREET ROULETTE

As a preface to the content of this book, I offer this information.

The most important function of this short book is to inform new investors that have little or no experience with the stock market aware of the availability of Paper-trading as a training tool and to itemize the many little hooks and pitfalls that new investors should be aware of before ever making a stock purchase with real money.

Much of the information offered here is what an experienced investor can read between the lines of most stock trading books. Without years of experience or constant conversations with experienced stock investors, the information here may never be revealed.

Do not expect a lot of drama and excitement in this books content.

Expect important guidelines for the novice investor that will help you hold your own and make responsible decisions in your stock equity purchases.

Wall Street Roulette is directed at the individual that has never traded stocks and novice traders with very little knowledge of investing in the stock markets.

Everything you find in this book is somewhere on the internet and in many other books.

With thousands of sources and excellent search engines, you will be able to simply type your question in your browser search request line and get a quick response to answer the questions you will have for definitions, explanations and strategies.

If someone were to ask me, what should I need to look for or watch out for? I would have to give him or her a copy of this book.

There are so many anomalies that can occur in the stock markets on a daily basis, it is best to start out with a routine that consistently alerts you to potential events for each stock in your portfolio each day.

Trading stocks requires work: the more you learn about trading stocks the better trader you can become.

In situations that I use a definition or explanation, I have used http://www.investopedia.com/   as the reference source.

Sign up for free newsletters at the Investopedia site.

I recommend that you go to the Investopedia website and research each new term that you do not understand or find a book with a complete set of investment related definitions.

The first of many rules to adhere to:

"Do not pray to the livestock, the Bull on Wall Street leaves much doubt in whether God would endorse stock trading anymore than praying to idols".

CHAPTER 2
TO DESCRIBE THE STOCK MARKET IS EASY FOR ME.

The Stock Markets are one of the most popular forms of legalized gambling available in the world. {What personalities do not realize as regards to the stock market is that it is truly a huge confidence game.} See reference below.

If this kernel of honesty turns you off and you never invest in the market, you have spent your money wisely.

If you have never traded stocks because you do not understand the Stock Market and how it works or you have been afraid to make the first steps to investing, I say "Be Afraid. Be Very Afraid". The stock market is very unforgiving; a simple case of "Fat Finger" can cost you. If you ever make an entry error, telephone your broker and get a correction immediately. Never depend on E-mail or delay in getting the correction made. Your broker knows people make entry errors and will not think you are a fool for getting an error corrected.

The more education you can get before you invest real money the better off you will be.

Investing in stocks is a lot like putting your money on a racehorse and watching him run against other horses, hoping that your horse will finish in the money.

One thing that is different from betting the horses is that your stock values often go up slightly or down slightly, in effect you can be a small winner with a small profit or a small looser and still be holding most of your money in your investment account at the end of each day. Losing it all on one stock in one day is rare unless you are buying penny stocks that are already in bankruptcy action or receivership.

It is a rare situation for a stock to soar to new highs in a single day but quite common for a stock value to drop significantly. The general scenario is; stocks go down faster than they go up.

To buy shares of stock you will pay a brokerage fee of about $10.00 (more or less) and you will pay a like fee to sell the stock when you exit the trade. The combination of both the buy and sell transactions is called a "Round Trip".

I have had trading months when the Brokerage Firm made more money from my trading account than I did since my stock roundtrips were so many and the profit margins so thin after paying their $20.00 round trip commissions. You need to experience this, so do not be frustrated when it happens. When you have mastered the Paper-Trading program and are ready to move onto real-time investing, you can move your account to a discount broker with very low execution fees and make hundreds more each month from the same trades.

{Here are sundry facts involving stockbrokers allowing real time Paper-trading.}

 I expect you will find it helpful since very good sources of understanding concerning stockbrokers allow real time Paper-trading may possibly at times be difficult to find.

What personalities do not realize as regards to the stock market is that it is truly a huge confidence game. Even after the stock market crash, people persist to believe that there is such a thing as a safe investment. Investing inside the NASDAQ stock market is under no circumstances safe. If you do not comprehend this, you should not play the stocks. Gimmicks akin to investing online lure a new generation of people with the promise of painless money. It is right that online investment bequeaths the possibility of easy money. Cash may be easily won or easily lost. In no way gamble with more than you may perhaps afford to lose!

If you crave to invest in the stock market, you should spend at least six months discovering it. Study everything that you can with reference to the stock market. Explore stock market history, probe economics, and peruse the advice of leading investors. It may well make sense for you to select a few stocks to follow closely. This will give you a concept of the vacillation of the stock market. Mainly, you should plunge yourself as deeply as you can in stocks before you fritter away any cash on them. It not at all makes sense to play a sport that you do not know for cash. It can only end badly.

I hope the first half of this essay gave you some helpful facts and figures concerning stockbrokers allow real time Paper-trading. Even though you were markedly searching for stock brokers allow real time Paper-trading, this piece of writing should prove fruitful. Keep reading.

I started investing in the NYSE stock market about six years ago, before I knew whatsoever I was doing. I had taken a few classes in economics, as well as had a solid mathematical background similarly. Overall, I thought I was hot stuff. I thought the stock market might be a cinch. Evidently, I was improper. I eventually broke even, as well as even turned a profit. In the first year or two, however, I lost massive amounts of cash. The stock market plunged me deeply into financial debt. I was much more qualified than many starting investors; however, I still was cleaned out.

Unluckily, I am afraid that my counsel about the stock market will maybe set out unheeded. Men and women seem to need to make their own errors. No person wants to hear a safe message of caution as well as forethought. Individuals frequently like to listen to the person who says that they may get rich quickly. You would get wealthy quick on the stock market; however, you might get poor even faster.

At present we have come to the end of this information with reference to stockbrokers providing real time Paper-trading. Reference: http://www.stocks-tradings.com/stock-brokers-allow-real-time-paper-trading.html }

As you progress in your study of the stock market, you should parallel your education with some trading activities in the Paper-trading program you have chosen. Try out some short sales, equity purchases and any and many potential opportunities that your continuing education may cause you to have questions. It is fortunate that you have the Paper-trading platform to exercise your curiosities.

CHAPTER 3
BEFORE YOU INVEST A PENNY

The stock market and stocks, bonds, options, derivatives are a viable solution to enhance or build personal retirement programs.

In the history of 401K programs, they have had many benefits for any Mutual Fund manager but few for the individual investor. Request a list of the fees and charges relating to your Mutual fund and 401K plan. You will be surprised when you find that the Mutual

Fund Manager makes more from your retirement account than you ever will.

New legislation in 2011 will require disclosure of all fees related to your 401K (full details are not out 9/1/2011). To improve 401(k) transparency.

This provision was part of H.R. 4213, The American Jobs and Closing Tax Loopholes Act of 2010.

You may have to be assertive and question if there are any hidden or undisclosed fees relating to your account such as entry fees, transaction fees, accounting fees, exit fees, monitoring fees, reporting fees, information inquiry fees etc.

At the very least get their (current) company brochure and locate the plan you are enrolled in, study it carefully and then ask the questions you have by personal phone call to the company. (You do not want a canned speech or a universal reply form called a FYI from their website.)

You are entitled to know which stocks, bonds and other investments are in your plan, along with monthly reporting on transactions that change the list.

If you are new to stock trading, use the information provided in this small book to "Paper Trade" stocks.

Use the information provided here to form good research habits related to Paper-trading stocks.

I make no guarantees about the effectiveness of these suggestions but say now, "Use the information only in a Paper-trading scenario!" If you decide to proceed into real time investment of your own funds before having a full six months of Paper-trading you are a brave soul.

If you set your business plan and your goal to Paper Trade for six months, you will probably experience both a great market upward explosion and a flash crash.

You must have real time quotes to learn trading strategies.

Involvement in the buying and selling process is mandatory and trading through a paper-trading program is about the only way to get safe hands on experience that will lead you to a better understanding of the transaction process.

Without emersion in the process of trading you would soon find that watching stock tickers, charts and news is about as exciting as watching grass grow.

Most Paper-trading programs will have approximately a 20-minute delay; however there are Paper-trading programs through many brokers that have real time quotes and streaming quotes if you have deposited money with them and have active trading authority with their firm. Do not waste your time with any trading programs that do not have real-time quotes and executions on your orders.

Search out a brokerage that has real-time quotes in their paper-trading platforms.

Typing Real Time Stock Trading into the Google search line will get you a list of potential platforms from many brokerages.

Ask the broker if his charting software will allow following streaming quotes of after hours or pre-market trades. You will need this function.

CHAPTER 4
YOUR ATTITUDE

As you start each day, watching your stock purchases increase and decrease in value, you will question what is really happening here.

In a great number of cases' the buyers of large blocks of stock are not buying with their own funds. Often they are fund managers filling orders to satisfy monthly buying requirements for 401K investment packages. They buy enough volume to make stocks values move and there is no possible way for you to know when this event is happening.

The market and all the stocks move each day in value as they trade. If a stock becomes stagnant, the Market Maker for that stock will buy shares that his company will hold for a period and then sell. Each stock in the major exchanges has a Market Maker assigned to it. Low value stocks traded as Over the Counter or Pink Sheets have a market maker and can purchase or sell to create liquidity in the stock. Be careful when selecting stocks, be sure that they have good daily volume or you may be holding stagnant stocks in your portfolio. Even if you reduce your asking price, you may have to wait for a sale.

http://www.investopedia.com search the term market maker.

If you are stuck in a stock and cannot get out because you are emotionally bound into staying, you can easily be starting the "Death by one thousand paper cuts".

There have been a few examples that I have personally experienced and I must relate that it is truly like a thousand cuts when you sit each day watching your wall of pain (computer screen).

As each moment, passes you expect to see News that made the stock react as you are witnessing the up- tick and down- tick.

I must sincerely admit that this one crisis investment error has brought me closer to God.

I can thank Green Mountain Coffee Roasters for bringing my Christian life into my full view for the first time.

While suffering the pain of a thousand paper cuts I had to reassure myself with the following thoughts.

Do not make quick judgments.

Turn crisis into opportunity.

Deal with anger immediately.

Refuse to give way to changing feelings.

I had become spoiled by many years of success in trading profitably and this time I behaved recklessly in throwing my investment capitol around like I had no appreciation for the God given blessings that had played a big part in my prior successes.

After many years of successful stock trading, I made one of the mistakes that I always warn every new investor to avoid.

The rule I ignored : Set an exit strategy.

Because I failed to set rules for exiting, I rode an emotional roller coaster for over 180 days while sitting on a position I sold short on GMCR.

I was a true example of stubbornness, greed, ignorance and complacency.

I sold the stock short at $37.81 and watched it climb to over $96.00 per share. My one redeeming feature was that I was only in for one hundred shares.

My losses mounted up to over six thousand dollars before I finally found relief from my many days experiencing the death by a thousand paper cuts.

You can experience a sample of the thousand paper cuts by revisiting the GMCR year to date chart and seeing my stock short sale on Feb 3 2011 at 2:37 PM and following it through July 29 2011.

The chart covering these dates is the history that represents my death by over five thousand paper cuts.

Since GMCR was under SEC investigation for cooking their books by falsifying twenty-two million in earnings (claimed through a math error), I stayed in the stock hoping for the information to come forward before or on the July 27th 2011 earnings report by GMCR.

In my wildest dreams, I just never expected that analyst would continue to pump the stock with the SEC still investigating the company.

I had a chance to get out at only three hundred and fifty dollars loss the day after my short sale but stayed in the investment out of pure greed because I had recently made a profit on exactly the same short sale transaction. I incorrectly expected the same results with this transaction.

So as I have stated before, never buy a position without an exit strategy firmly attached to your transaction order.

Never allow your stock investments to rely on your emotional state. Set the rules for entry, exit with the initial stock purchase, and be done with it. You will sleep better and can go off to work without the fear that follows a questionable transaction, as all stock purchases and even stock sales are.

I can now say that although my losses were in the range of five thousand dollars I would rather have a five thousand dollar loss in one day and avoid that five thousand cuts scenario again spread out over the one-hundred and eighty days.

Setting an exit strategy is your way to avoid excruciating pain over an extended time.

If you are experiencing anxiety or sleepless nights, working in the Paper-trading program you should close you account and go back to your real life.

If you are intent to stay active in stock trading, never discuss your results with anyone else. If you enter into conversations with any other trader, you will find out, everybody is more qualified, smarter, bigger earners than you are.

Conversations about your stock trading activities seldom leads to anything other than frustration and disappointment in your results that lead to insecurity in your selections of stocks in your portfolio.

Investing money (real or imagined) can be a very personal thing that you do not want to make public to friends and family members.

If your Paper-trading portfolio makes you look like a big failure, you should wipe out all positions by resetting your account, get a fresh start by following your game plan of setting limits on every transaction, and suppress your ego.

Buying on the shotgun example of throwing darts at the newspaper stock pages seldom works as well as proper research. You just cannot remove the work required to be successful.

Freedom of choice is a wonderful thing and you absolutely should take many "Flyers", dream buys on any stock hunch or gut feeling that comes upon you. Behaving irresponsibly, acting on your ego, acting on greed is a great experience that will all lead you back to doing it the hard but proper way of researching before you decide to buy.

Once you move onto trading with real money, you should take cash out of your trading account on a regular basis when you have profits. It is nice to see the portfolio grow past your original investment but taking the cash reminds us that this is real money. Buying something with the cash you take out is better than just letting it set in your bank account, it further sets the understanding that the account is real money and deserves a great deal of respect.

When you move onto real money trades, if you are investing for long-term gains, you should have a separate account folder for stocks you have purchased as long-term investments. Removing the temptation for quick profits will ease your anxiety. Any investment for over a year is long-term.

CHAPTER 5
THE DANGEROUS PATH TO DAY TRADING

What qualifies a person as a pattern day trader?

Many persons reading this book may be saying "Whoa! This guy is getting the cart before the horse."

I have intentionally started with this information because I know how emotional new traders are when they start making money or losing money on stocks.

There is nothing wrong with grabbing a quick profit or dumping a stock to reduce potential losses but the investor needs to be aware of the looming problems if you do it on a daily basis.

As of Sept 28, 2001, the NASD (now, FINRA) and NYSE amended their definitions of day traders. A new term that they use is "pattern day trader". An investor can be classified as a pattern day trader by having one of the two following characteristics:

1.He or she makes day round trip trades four or more times during a five-day span, or

2.The firm where the investor is making transactions, or opening up a new account, reasonably considers him or her a day trader

Once an investor is considered a day trader, the brokerage must classify him or her as such, and the investor is then subject to increased equity requirements. Mainly, the brokerage must require a minimum equity of $25,000 at the beginning of the customer's trading day. This minimum equity requirement has been introduced by the Securities & Exchange Commission and the NYSE. Ensuring that any substantial losses can be offset by the day trader's own equity, the requirement addresses the inherent risk imposed on brokerages by leveraged day trading activities.

A more restrictive margin rule has also been implemented. Day traders are permitted to purchase only four times their maintenance margin levels. If this level is exceeded, the firm must issue a margin call to the day trader who subsequently has five business days to deposit the funds before the account is halted from additional trading. Reference: http://www.investopedia.com search the term Day Trader

Depending on the profits and / or losses, you may want to exit a trade the same day you buy in.

If you sell this position within the same trading day, you are flagged as a potential Day Trader with one flag attached to your trading account. If you make the daily exiting of positions a routine practice and have four round trips in a trading week (5 days) you will be tagged as a Pattern Day trader. It is important that you know what your activities are leading you to.

A pattern day trader will have "restrictions" on his / her account. The first of these is the requirement to have $25,000.00 cash (can vary by brokerage) and or equities value in your account at the start of the trading day.

If your morning opening cash and equities are less the restriction can cause your trading account to be frozen until you bring your cash / equity values up to the $25,000.00 minimum. If your account balance falls below the daily minimum, the brokerage firm will notify you automatically after market close for the day that you must fund your account to remove the restrictions before you can initiate a buy trade on the following day.

When you add money to your account, it can take several days to complete the transaction. This delay can be a killer for your stock portfolio.

When the restriction is active, it prohibits you from opening a position (buying stocks / options etc. until the minimum is again in your account.)

You will still be able to sell stocks from your account to bring in cash or to exit a position that may or may not represent a loss.

Never feel that you cannot exit a stock if it is going against you. If you have fallen victim to irrational trading or gotten caught by your exit triggers you can always sell your stock position.

If it is your first time to be labeled a pattern day trader, you can call your brokerage firm, and explain the situation. They have the authority to reset your account if you have a responsible reason for the accidental action.

Avoid canceling pending orders. If you have placed a buy limit order at less than the current market price and see that the stock is falling quickly and can go below your limit buy price you can edit your buy order price down and save a cancellation fee or buy at the lower price if it reaches your new lower offer.

CHAPTER 6

WHAT IS THE GOAL WHEN YOU START YOUR INVESTMENT BUSINESS PLAN?

I think universally our goal is to make money. There needs to be some attainable goals defined.

I have entered my own information here for your consideration.

I entered with $50,000.00 and without any plan I miraculously earner $19,000.00 between July 2007 and December 2007 Tax reporting. I consider that as purely a miracle and dumb luck because I entered in a market that was bouncing 300 points each day on the DOW index.

During the second reporting year, I earned another $11,000.00 with very little effort.

The third year I earned about $12,000.00 with very little effort.

My portfolio very seldom increased over the original $50,000.00 for more than the few days it took me to transfer my profits out by electronic transaction process "ACH".

At the end of the fourth year, I was still holding about $50,000.00 in the account but only earned and withdrawn $9,000.00.

During the first seven months of the fifth year I took $25.000.00 in losses. I can attribute that to several "Flash Crashes" in the first part of 2011.

I must admit I let myself get greedy and let my ego over ride my business plan.

There were several days that I earner over $3,000.00 and several days I lost as much as $7,000.00 in a single day. The losses were in

OPTIONS Trading where all your money goes, like pulling the handle of a slot machine.

I made the single most common mistake that many traders make. I thought I was smart.

I let my ego, greed and impatience gain control of my trading.

In my hindsight it is quite clear to me that trading equities has much less risk than trading options.

I have learned my lesson and I am back purely trading Equities where there is less risk if you stay with a firm trading plan.

I made all of the profits by taking the $50.00 or $100.00 on almost every stock transaction I made. It took a lot of trades in the $750.00 to $2000.00 purchase range and the broker made a nice profit because the trades were thin on profit and very numerous.

One of the most important things I learned from the first year of trading was; do not begrudge the broker his commissions. I made money, the broker made money. Without the trading platform and account management provided by the broker, I would have been stuck in a 3% CD all year.

I never worked with a Paper-trading program until 2010. I have traded with my real time account and practiced with the Paper-trading programs since early 2010.

I know now that I probably had a great burning desire to fail when I started trading my real money immediately with very little stock market knowledge.

Take my advice!

Do not trade with real money until you can be profitable for several months in a Paper-trading scenario.

CHAPTER 7
SETTING EXIT LIMITS ON YOUR STOCK PURCHASES

Every business should start out with a business plan. Often the original plan needs to be up-dated or modified; however, the original plan should be allowed to prove itself before you start making major changes. The term, measurable results applies here.

Your business plan in stock trading centers around rigid rules of buying and selling stocks at preset amounts. Follow the preset order placement and exit guidelines for a reasonable time before you start thinking you are smarter than the professional that work on the strict guidelines exemplified below.

Almost every brokerage firm that offers electronic trading provides you with the real time computer software to manage your trading account and a Paper-trading account with purchasing and selling, tracking you account cash, margins etc.

Along with the purchasing and selling, they have Order Entry Options that you can set as defaults or customize as you enter a stock purchase. The order area of the program will allow you to set limits that will automatically sell your stock if it drops down to your stop limit or sell your stock if it reaches your desired sell point. In most cases, you can go back after your basic order has been entered and modify your initial settings or add the stop limit sale or a sell to take profit order if you purchase without setting these with your placement of your basic order.

For those investors that are not going to spend every trading day watching their portfolio the initial entry into trading stocks through your Paper-trading program set your sell trigger at $50.00 profit no matter how big the transaction, get used to taking money anytime there is fifty dollars on the table.

The exit triggers your sell price. If you are sitting in front of your computer and you have a chance to take $30.00 you should over-ride the trigger and take a profit. If you are within a few nickels or dimes of reaching that $30.00 do not wait for those pennies, sell now.

The trigger settings protect you but opportunity to take a profit is the deciding factor in all stock transactions. Trading stocks is a for profit endeavor and regardless of the transaction profit the stock will still be there tomorrow and it could be at a lower price than you previously paid. It is quite common to place swing trades and buy the same stock several times a week.

The purpose of trading with a Paper-Trading Program is to learn how to set up the order pre-sets in the software, how set up watch lists and how to execute orders.

While you are trading in the Paper-Trading Program it is important that you learn to "let go" and sell your stocks at a small profit and sell at a loss if that is the case. Holding out for the big profits often passes that magic $50.00 profit and drops rapidly into lesser profit ranges. If you over-ride, your sell trigger at the $50.00 mark and your stock starts down, do not stay with it, sell it immediately. There will be times when the stock recovers quickly and runs up well over the $50.00 profit taking range but it is important that you get accustomed to taking profits as soon as possible and this involves overcoming your emotions.

You can always look back with your 20 / 20 recall and regret selling too soon but selling too soon with a profit is better than staying too long watching your stock spiral down in flames and losses.

It is important that you fully understand how to set up your software to your defaults and or customize each order as you make the initial purchase of the stocks.

Stop loss orders. This is key. No investor should trade stocks without using stop loss orders. Most online brokerage firms do not offer stop loss orders on OTC stocks in the penny stock class.

I cannot stress the importance of stop loss orders enough. No investor should trade without them.

There are Electronic Trading Houses that buy big blocks of stocks and sell on very tight constraints. An example of stock purchases in the ranges of $300.00 up per share the exit strategy is to buy heavy and exit with only 2 or 3 % in profits but keep going back into the stock when it drops back to the original purchase price or below.

With unlimited capitol to invest, they can trade on a quarter % and still make money when the transactions are large. A purchase of 1000 shares of XYZ at $300.00 stock is profitable if the stock only moves five cents ($50.00). Although a move of 5% would make a $15,000.00 profit.

As you work with your Paper-trading program, you should try a few of these "Big Buys" and get the feel for sudden losses that can easily happen in large transactions.

CHAPTER 8
WHAT IS A STOP-LOSS ORDER?

It is an order placed with a broker to buy or sell once the stock reaches a certain price. A stop-loss is designed to limit an investor's loss on a security position. Setting a stop-loss order for 10% below the price at which you bought the stock will limit your loss to 10%. For example, let us say you just purchased Microsoft (NASDAQ:MSFT) at $20 per share. Right after buying the stock, you enter a stop-loss order for $18. This means that if the stock falls below $18, your shares will then be sold at the prevailing market price.

Reference: http://www.investopedia.com search the term stop loss

CHAPTER 9
WHAT DOES STOP-LIMIT ORDER MEAN?

An order placed with a broker that combines the features of stop order with those of a limit order. A stop-limit order will be executed at a specified price (or better) after a given stop price has been reached. Once the stop price is reached, the stop-limit order becomes a limit order to buy (or sell) at the limit price or better. Reference: http://www.investopedia.com/terms/s/stop-limitorder.asp

It is very important that you understand and practice entering and exiting stock purchases in your paper-trading program before you ever trade your first stock in real time with real money.

Each investor sees the world a little differently and approaches risk differently so it will be your decision as to the settings you prefer as a safety net in exiting trades gone bad or exiting profitable positions without daily minute-to-minute monitoring requirements.

It is very common for an active investor to be in twenty-five stocks. You can be at work and the sell to stop loss or sell to take profits triggers are on your account working for you.

Many brokers will not accept buy / sell triggers on stocks of value of less than $1.00. These stocks are often OTC / BBs (Over the Counter / Bulletin Board stocks).

Online brokerage firms can offer stop loss orders on OTC stocks but seldom provide them on stocks valued at less than $1.00.

This exclusion can also happen if your stock drops below the board requirements and are delisted from New York or NASDAQ, or OTC /BB board.

If you have bought one or more of the stocks in your portfolio at market open, it could very well hit one of your limits and close your position the same day while you are at work or not watching the market events unfold.

You may set restrictions on selling or buying in After Hours or Pre Market Hours of trading so your orders will not sell before or after standard trading hours. Most brokerages extend after hours trading privileges to all clients.

However, your stock trigger could activate on the morning bell if the stock has had lots of movement in the pre market or after hours trading session.

You can set trade triggers in your trading software that will not activate in after hours or pre-market hours of trading.

Make yourself aware of After Market and Pre-Market activity on your stocks. Your trade trigger could be activated at opening bell or closing bell at market price.This could be strike one towards Pattern Day Trader status, if your presets sell two stocks you purchased the same day. that of course is two and so forth throughout the day. It would be a rare thing for presets to put you into the day trader restrictions unless you set your limits very tight on many stocks that you purchased at market open on the day the triggers are activated. As an alternate, the presets could sell your stock and buy it again at a lower price, depending on how you set your order presets.

Any stock that you hold overnight and sells on your triggers or you initiate a sale the following day makes the trade called a swing trade that has no bearing on the day trader flag system.

Always enter your trades as Limit Orders. With the new electronic trading on all exchanges, it will not delay your order execution.

Being flagged as a day trader is not a death sentence but it can lock you out of potentially profitable trades that you cannot enter because of the restrictions. (Because you cannot open / buy a position while the restriction is active). While in your Paper-trading program, you may never be shut out for behaving like a Pattern Day Trader because your account will have more than the required $25,000.00 to qualify. You should keep yourself aware of the day trade count for your own information.

You'll be able to identify with these events after a few months of Paper-trading experience watching stock graphs and following news stories that make stocks move up or down during the average day.

Start Watch Lists in your Paper-trading program and keep track of stocks that have good or bad news that interest you. A watch list named "good news" works well for those qualifying and a watch list named "Bad News" for the bad boys falling down.

Never trust your memory: Keep watch list, Internet Links and note pads.

Disregard news that is older than 24 hours. Any movement caused by that news event has already happened. Do a quick check of your symbol stock chart to see the results of that news.

Stock charts are very important histories of any stock that has traded and can be an invaluable source of information. Although the media and stock tipsters may pump stocks, lie about earnings, they cannot change history that is in the charts.

Charts are about the only truth you will always be able to depend on when you are researching stocks.

Stock charts and the studies related to them is an important area worth educating yourself on.

Often trading platforms, even Paper-trading software has built in options to set up study groups that relate to your investment goals.

CHAPTER 10
MARGIN ACCOUNTS

When you buy on margin, you are borrowing money from your broker to buy stocks through his brokerage. You will be charged interest on the amount you borrow on margin even when you have the stock you just purchased as collateral.

If you apply for a margin account, along with a $10,000.00 account you are often blessed with a margin trading account equal to as much as two / four times the value of your cash plus the margin value of your equity stocks. (The margin amount is adjusted on a daily basis by the brokerage firm). You will have to request a margin account to activate margin buying but be aware of the pitfalls before you fill out the required forms.

You should read and understand these forms even if you do not intend to request a margin account. (You will probably have margin privileges with your paper-Trading account).

If you use all your cash buying equities or options your account then moves into buying on margin if you've requested a margin account.

Options contracts on stock positions seldom have margin value so be aware that your account can go into margin funds quickly if you are buying, many option contracts.

If you are shorting stocks and the stock moves against you (increases in value), it can cause your account to move into margin very quickly.

When you buy on margin, you are borrowing money to invest.

When you are SHORT SELLING, you are borrowing stock but still it is like borrowing the cash value in real money.

Read and understand the Term Short Float. In an abbreviated explanation, it means that if the short float is reported at 25%, it means that investors betting that the stock will be going down in value temporarily own 25% of the total outstanding stocks. They have temporarily borrowed these stocks from their brokers.

CHAPTER 11
OPENING YOUR NEW BROKERAGE ACCOUNT

Initially you will open a trading account with a cash deposit.

Depending on the broker, this can be from Zero cash on up to many thousands of dollars.

You should exercise some caution in selecting a brokerage firm that meets your needs.

Keep in mind that initially you'll only be Paper-trading so selecting a brokerage that offers real time quotes in Paper-trading is more a priority than the per trade price.

Incentives like "Free trades for 30 Days" or "Discount trade fees" are common for real time trades. You will have no fees associated with Paper-trading but you will see the Soft Money expenses as you buy and sell stocks.

Many brokerage accounts do not track the "Soft Money" that is paid in commissions on your daily transactions reporting but you need to be aware of the price of your roundtrip.

Text notifications to your Smart Phone or PDA are available from most trading platforms. Search the instructions for alerts and notices and set these up to track your transactions when you are not available at your computer.

In our modern high tech world, you will find that many brokerages have a condensed trading platform you can down load to your SmartPhone, Tablet, PDA and set up to track the general condition of your portfolio.

CHAPTER 12
CONSIREATIONS BEFORE BUYING A STOCK

The excitement of seeing the line, bar or candlestick of a stock graph climbing up at a rapid rate on a stock is common for new investors.

Great stock pickers are rare so the investor must overcome the desire for making big profits and get control of picking stocks very early on in their investment program.

Here are a few of the first things to consider:

1) Most purchases of equity stocks are in blocks of 100, although you can buy as few as one share. It would be difficult to realize a profit on a $39.00 stock purchased as a single stock when your round trip brokerage fees are deducted. If you brokerage charges $10.00 for buying a stock and $10.00 for selling the same stock, your stock would have to increase 100% in value for you to break even. Has this stock ever been as high as $59.00 within the past year? FYI, brokerage fees are called SOFT MONEY by many brokerages and do not appear on stock value reports that you view on screen. This must be considered if you are just dumping stock hoping to avoid a loss or you set tight

limits on stop loss sell or sell orders. You can potentially take losses you had not planned for on either side.

2) Work on the principal of KISS, "Keep it simple stupid". In the beginning, buy stocks that you could actually afford if you were investing your own money in a trading account. Consider that you will be buying 100 shares of each stock. That will exclude you from buying 100 shares of the highflying sweetheart stocks in the $300 / $400 range that get favorable mention on the open of every morning newscast.

3) When you are considering buying a stock you should look at the chart for one-year / one-month / one-week / one-day past performance for the stock, include after-hours and pre-market hours trading in the weekly and daily charts. It may have been up the required 50% from today's price or may have never exhibited to potential for a breakeven price. If possible, with the brokerage software you are using set the chart view to show after-hours and pre market trading.

4) A little quick calculator work can qualify this as a potential profitable trade or a looser. In other words, know what this stock must do to make you a profit if you buy it today. (I use an EXCEL page for this and can test a few dozen stocks just by plugging them into my preformatted EXCEL page).

5) Keep a calculator handy on your desktop. Leaving your chart, streaming quotes or breaking your concentration to pop-up the Windows Calculator is an unnecessary distraction.

6) Based on past history consider the current price and consider the potential for the stock to go down in value to a one year low and cause a loss. Know the 52-week high and the 52-week low.

7) Check the reaction of the stock on the dates the company reports on earnings and consider if the stock value escalates in favorable reported earnings or increase in any dividends that it may pay. Set reminders in your calendar program to track these activities.

8) If the FED chairperson is going to speak or other reports such as Labor, Agriculture, Energy reports are scheduled during the day, avoid entering any position until you see the impact of their report on the market or the sector in discussion.

9) Understand and use Book Value principals http://www.investopedia.com search the term book value.

10) ALERT! ALERT! When the DOW index market exhibits a FLASH CRASH of over a hundred points in one day, do not rush to trade. The crash often continues for several days and during the Flash Crash or within 48 hours, buying stocks is often a bad choice.

11) Use your Paper-trading software to experience this yourself. Buy all the stocks you have dreamed of owning and watch the results. If you can buy during the day when everything is declining you will be able to experience the meaning of catching a falling knife.

12) That is your very simplest research before even considering buying a stock.

13) Making that first trade http://www.investopedia.com search the term first trade.

CHAPTER 13
BUYING TO SPECULATE ON SHORT TERM GAINS

1) If you are investing with the intent of buying in a dip and selling on a high, you are among millions of traders.
2) There are other things to consider and you should include this research in your buying decision.
3) Check out the "Upcoming Events" of a stock, this includes the dates when dividends are paid if there are any. The dates that quarterly earnings reports are released and earnings report telephone calls are scheduled.
   http://biz.yahoo.com/research/earncal/
4) Check out past events of stocks, this will provide valuable information such as the up down movement at the time the company reported quarterly earnings, increased dividends, reduced dividends. Events such as acquisitions or sales of various holdings are also important in buying decisions.
5) Check out Insider-Trading (stocks / interest) sold by major stockholders within the company.
6) Check out Institutional positions in the stock with buys and the dates with related events of the stock.

7) Check to see if there were insider stock sales at or near the IPO date of the stock if it is a recent IPO.

8) Monitor daily volume relative to price changes on cheap stocks be aware large price jumps on small volume sales is deceiving. A big jump on cheap stocks often indicates a pump and dump scam is active on that stock.

9) Check out Pre-Market and After Hours trading on stocks you are considering.

10) Just as soon as the market opens for the day, check to see what the sector is doing that contains the stock that you are considering. Often the whole sector containing 20 or more stocks goes up and down at the same time with only one or two stocks exhibiting a breakout pattern that could possibly make them interesting candidates for a buy scenario.

11) Log onto NASDAQ Level II and monitor real-time transactions. Monitor after Hours and Pre Market trading at the Nasdaq site http://www.nasdaq.com/quotes/after-hours.aspx

CHAPTER 14
BUYING STOCK TO HOLD FOR LONG-TERM GAINS

1) History on all stocks can tell us a great deal but do not just look at the charts and make assumptions; you still need to look at the performance of the stock. Use all of the research available to you in making your buy / sell decision.

2) Some sectors are on fast pace and represent riskier investment strategies. Other sectors are slowly disappearing down the drain. Many sectors perform well in season but fall off sharply after the season.

3) Check out the dividends paid if there are any and make yourself a review schedule for each stock you are following or that you own. (Keep a calendar and set alerts for a day ahead of the event date).
4) The dividend information is usually linked to future events dates related to earnings.
5) Keep your long-term investments in a separate portfolio to avoid the temptation to take quick profits.
6) Keep track of the dividends and dividend dates on your long-term investments. Dividend stocks are great long-term investments.

CHAPTER 15
MOVING ON THE NEWS

Television news reporters that work for the major TV and cable news stock related feeds are not allowed to own stocks / bonds etc. (I don't know if they are monitored) They are paid indirectly through advertizing revenues by the most powerful brokerage firms in the world. They are "Talking Heads"; they just repeat the words fed through headphone sets and Teleprompters. They speak like knowledgeable investors but they are not.

They can be more dangerous than you may imagine because they can take a simple statement coming through the headphones and put their own spin on it making it quite attractive when in reality it might be negative news.

The purpose of their reporting position is to encourage the viewers to make a stock transaction. Brokers win on both sides with commission payable at the buy transaction and on the sell transaction. Do not get caught up in the news reporter's enthusiasm in your decisions to purchase stocks.

There are charismatic news reporters just as there are charismatic ministers and politicians. Never let yourself get charmed into buying a "Sweetheart Stock" that is being pumped by one of the "Talking Heads" that fill the reporter's seats.

One of the first things to remember when researching the news on any stock: Always check the date of the News Release. The internet captures and holds a wealth of information and the search process brings up old news along with the current news.

Almost all NYSE and NASDAQ stocks that trade over two million shares a day will have movement related to market news stories about them as exceptional movement occurs or an important event happens and gets a mention on news channels or gets distributed by financial news services.

You cannot expect news every day but there will be four quarterly earnings reports and dividend announcements each year that will most often encourage a change in stock value through increased volume. This can be an up move or a down move relative to good news or bad news. Many stocks have radical moves just prior or just after the quarterly earnings report.

Likewise, it could be a stock that just stays flat because it is a stable company that seldom had increased quarterly profits or changes the dividends it pays to stockholders.

OTC/BB stocks can trade in the millions and not have news reporting. You can go to the OTCBB website and get news releases on selected stocks.

Do not get caught up in penny stocks that have huge volume increases for a few days. The stocks often go up in value by large percentages but in most situations they represent a buyer beware scenario because somebody is running a pump and dump scheme using that stock. You will want to trade in stocks with a volume of one million or more on most days, it gives the stock liquidity in selling the stock quickly if you want to get out and move on.

Stocks that trade small volume can be stagnant and you can get caught holding stocks that you no longer want to own waiting for a buyer. These small volume stocks are often small companies that seldom have news about them that will create buy / sell activity.

You will want to know how much dividend a stock pays, the date you must own it to get the dividend and how the dividend is paid, quarterly, semi-annually or annually.

You will also want to know the ex-dividend date, which is the last date you can purchase a stock and partake of the dividend. It is a small thing on small stocks but can be considerable on expensive stocks that pay substantial dividends or on stocks that you own in great volume. The ex-dividend date can be a deciding factor in purchasing some stocks for many investors.

The news you do not get is the stock purchases / sales in high volume by Institutional investors that can move the market value of a stock.

When reporters are discussing volatility it is often relative to the activities of institutional and investment fund traders. You will hear their exclamations that the market is going up or going down and they are not aware of an anomaly to cause this action. You will see this very often when the markets make substantial increases or decreases without credible news releases to encourage the market.

In addition, you should check the insider trading on any stock you are considering buying or selling. Often the VIP's with companies sell off large blocks of stock when the stocks hit a new high or buy in (take earned shares) when the stocks drop substantially or hit a new low.

News of acquisitions can make a stock value move. The movements on either side of the acquisition companies can make substantial moves that are transient, creating only a few minute blips on the stock value prior to the announcement.

Sometimes potential acquisitions are announced that never reach completion or may be delayed for other reasons but cause unwarranted value changes in the underlying stocks on both sides of the proposed acquisition. Use caution in acting on news items about mergers and acquisitions, the news is sometimes only rumors that are picked up and delivered by reputable news providers that think the news is authentic.

When you research stocks always read any news item that contains the word "Correction" or "Deleted Press Release", in the first line. You will be surprised how many of these you can see each day.

As part of your Paper-trading, you should make a few purchases of stocks on underlying companies offered for sale or have mergers and acquisitions news currently fresh.

Analyst news is something you need to keep a close eye on. The Analyst reports are not released on a predictable schedule but you can do a quick search on Analyst upgrades / downgrades first thing each morning through Yahoo Finance and get reliable information.

Analyst are contractors for the Company that is paying them for their analysis and are using information provided by auditors that are also contractors for the company in question.

Over several months, you may find several analyst reports coming from more than one analyst on the same company and they may each have a completely differing opinion about the company.

You will also have news feeds supplied with your basic Brokerage Software that may have several analyst reports linked in.

Do not be surprised when you find disagreement among Analyst over the potential of an individual stock.

Get the news feeds on the stocks you own and review the news each morning. A quick morning search of upgrades and downgrades before market open will be a valuable tool since many analyst release ratings over weekends and long holiday weekends.

VERY IMPORTANT Always be certain that the stock you are following is the stock being discussed in news stories. Example (AMLM vs. AMEL) the name may be very similar and confusing.

Both companies are American Lithium but are not the same potential investment.

CHAPTER 16
NEWS, WHEN IT IS NOT NEWS

Often news comes in the form of restricted short selling that comes in the form of a tag or note on your stock portfolio or to one of your watch-lists. Flags can also indicate suspended trading when a stock had an earnings report due within the trading day, a stock split is in progress, and these restrictions can be set for a variety of reasons. You will just have to do some research to see how the restriction may affect you. One of the most important events related to one of the flags is when the company fails to file quarterly reports in a timely manner or has major accounting errors in the reports. Sometimes a flag will be a signal that trading is suspended on the stock.

On days with earnings reports after hours the suspended trading may only be about an hour and then it can be traded again after hours after suspension is lifted.

As part of the long learning curve, you should have a watch list on after hour's highest volume trading stocks and execute some after hour's trades on this list.

Be watchful for news or reports notifying the public of potential accounting errors, questionable accounting methods or suspected fraud in reporting documents and reports of SEC starting any type of investigation of the underlying stock and the company it represents. SEC can start investigations that are ongoing for over a year or more. It is best to avoid any stock that has ongoing investigations. A bad report arising from an investigation can cause the stock on that company to drop like a rock.

A history of failing to file the required SEC documents on a timely manner can be a red flag to pull out before the stock is delisted from the current exchange.

The SEC can delist a stock and prohibit it from trading. Prohibit it from trading can mean that it cannot be traded on US Stock markets even as a Bulletin Board or Over the counter Stock.

If you already own a stock that gets delisted, you will see the name of the stock change by the addition of one or two letters indicating that it is now a Bulletin board or over the counter traded stock.

If a stock is "removed from trading", it can have value but you cannot sell it until the stock is reinstated. Owning one or more of these stocks is frustrating because your money is locked down and you have no exit to get your money.

Periodically you will experience a stock event that greatly increases a single stock value in just a few minutes or over an hour or two. I think we can call this news one of two things, either the Buffet effect or the Steve Jobs effect. When Warren Buffet bought BAC warrants, the BAC stock sold for about $2.00 up from the prior day close but settled back at about $0.52 gain for the day. Still a nice increase on a $6.99 stock but if you had rushed to buy when the news was released you would be down from the $8.80 high for the day to a $7.60 low. You can research the BAC chart for August 25, 2011.

There are modern day spin-doctors on cable TV that interview company CEO's and CFO's on the air. Almost without exception, this scenario will cause a bump up in the underlying stock price the next day. Beware of buying on publicity! If you truly consider the source respectable and knowledgeable, try to wait 48 hours while watching the stock. You will in this action save more money than you lose by owning the stock later rather than sooner. You will find that other investment celebrities that make big stock buys or attempt to gain control of undervalued companies can move the market. It is best to maintain control of your emotions and watch the stock closely for the first dip and then consider buying on the second dip that eventually comes after the emotional and electronic traders are through in the second day.

Just because the celebrity investors can exhibit some control temporarily over the daily stock price on a single stock does not insulate them from losses that they never report to the news media. (As Celebrity investors come and go you will see them, rise and fall in News Media coverage).

CHAPTER 17
DAILY TIMING OF EVENTS

Market open and close times are stated in Eastern Standard Time.

Each day the European Market closes at 11:30 EST. It is good to watch all your stocks and see how they react to this important daily event. Since you will probably be at work, make a watch list of four stocks and each evening check the daily chart and see what they did at 11:30 AM. After a few of these previews, you will see the trend that transpires each day as the European Market closes. Part of what you want to track on these same four stocks is how they close at the end of the normal trading day at 4:00 PM EST.

Be particularly watchful on Fridays and any day when the NYSE and NASDAQ markets will be closed on the following day like Thanksgiving and any other National Holidays that may fall on Monday of the next week such as Labor Day.

Weekends that require the market to be closed on a normal Monday may have exceptional volume activity on the Friday before the closing bell. (Check the current list of Market Closed Dates, it can change.) Higher volume in stocks on Friday is often related to "Filling Shorts" or "Buying Shorts to Close Short Positions in Stocks". Stocks can often surge up late Friday afternoon before market closing because some investors cover short positions.

Weekends are quite unpredictable since wars start, terrorist events occur, earthquakes happen and many Analyst Reports come about on weekends.

After-hours trading transactions can have effects on your holdings.

Earnings reports can be released in the market day and are released before market hours and after market hours.

Changes in dividend payments (if there any) will be released with quarterly reports unless there has been some special event like a merger, stock split or special circumstances.

Earnings calls are telephone-reporting events that are conducted in the trading day that you can log onto and listen. Try this a few times to become knowledgeable about these events.

CHAPTER 18
SHORT SELLERS ATTEMPT TO SELL HIGH AND BUY LOW

Short sellers borrow shares from other investors, sell them on the open market, and buy back the same number of shares initially borrowed.

If the short seller can buy back the stock at a lower price, he turns a profit off the difference -- basically, he is betting on the stock to lose value.

Short-sellers take on unlimited risk because they (theoretically) have unlimited downside -- if the stock keeps rising, they keep losing, so they tend to be a bit more sophisticated than your average investor.

For this list, we wanted to focus on large cap stocks that have seen a significant decrease in shares shorted over the last month. Meaning that short sellers, who tend to be a little bit more sophisticated, seem to think the upside potential outweighs the downside potential.

Reference: http://seekingalpha.com/article/272707-short-squeeze-large-caps-stocks-with-significant-short-covering (June 1, 2011 report)

If the stock you are considering is on this short list of short seller favored stocks it indicates that the market on this stock is being moved by speculators and not investors such as mutual funds, retirement fund or other long term institutional investors. Beware of an exodus by short sellers that will drive this stock into the positive / negative very quickly. The exodus often happens during after- hours trading and on Fridays as Short Sellers get out before unpredictable events that can happen over weekends. Stocks can often surge up late Friday afternoon before market closing because of investors buying to cover short positions and can continue into afterhours trading.

This Friday surge in either direction is usually not news related, with the exception of a company reporting quarterly earnings at or near closing hour. You will need to check the upcoming events for the subject stock each time you want to confirm this notable change in stock performance.

You should approach short selling with great fear!

Short selling is one of the few things that can completely wipe out your stock portfolio in just a few hours. Most short sales involve stocks in increments of one hundred shares. The math is easy when you work with blocks of round numbers since the underlying stock price and the upward trend is calculator by multiples of one hundred.

Making several trades in your paper-trading program can provide you with a wealth of experience. Set one Short sale transaction with a stop loss and set another transaction without the stop loss and you will see immediate educational benefits of avoiding Short Selling and the results of not setting stop loss on your orders.

Many times news comes out Pre-market and After-hours. This news can take a heavy toll on your stock values if you are not watching. As a rule, most investors do not follow the market outside normal trade hours.

CHAPTER 19
THE ROUTE TO FOLLOW

First things first.

Set up an additional E-mail box to send all financial information junk mail to before you go any farther. You will not want all this spam and junk mail to route to your cell phone or your important personal mailbox / company mailbox or shared family mailbox.

Locate a brokerage that has real-time streaming quotes in their paper- trading program, make your initial $ deposit into the real account to have access to the Paper-trading Software. Start learning the Paper-Trading software by watching any training videos offered in the Paper-trading or real-time trading software. Even if the Paper-trading software does not have the full features of the Real Time software, it will still be a very important learning activity.

If you have never worked with Brokerage Software Platform, you are in for a real treat. There is always lots of activity on your screen or screens. There are streaming quotes, news flash pop-ups, colorful graphs and even cable channel stock-market news feeds.

Almost as quickly as you sign up with a brokerage account you will start getting offers for financial tip sheets, free training seminars, free penny trading tip sheets just as soon as you get your first Paper-trading Account set up. Set the default portfolio investment at the lowest value that is practical. Having a million or two is great but you will need the Paper Money Availability set at a reasonable amount that will cause you some concern when you start and help you learn some caution.

1. Learn the Order Entry systems and set up your defaults for Stop Limit settings and Sell Triggers within the order entry program of the Paper-trading program. Set the defaults up even if you do not fully understand what you are doing, you can always change the settings as you learn more. On a ten-dollar stock that you purchase 100 shares, 10% is a reasonable stop loss setting, on that same ten-dollar stock a 25% gain is not a reasonable sell point for a trade trigger if that stock has not reached that value within the last 52 weeks. Consider a $360.00 stock that you own 100 shares; a 2% stop loss might be more practical 5% or $50.00 sell for profit can be applied. Generally, in training scenario I set all Stop Limit Sell orders to sell the stock anytime I can take a $50.00 profit on the transaction. (This is very practical when you are purchasing less than $5000.00 in a single stock under $20.00 per share). You can make your own rules as you get more educated but always remember have an exit strategy in place that is not based on your emotions or flash reactions to the stock movements during the trading day.

2. After you trade the top ten stocks for a few days, you will get a better feel for how you want to apply your safety nets. As a reasonable entry-strategy try to set all your sell triggers to activate and execute when your stock has reached $50.00 profit.

   That may sound a little strange but when you are trading in the real world a fifty or hundred dollar profit on a stock is a viable criterion to sell and take profits. After all a hundred dollars could pay your cell phone bill, TV cable bill, take two people out to dinner, buy a couple of tanks of gas or buy a nice gift for someone you care for.

3. Set up the charts to show the following STUDIES:
    A: Bollinger Bands B: Keltner Channel
    C: On Balance Volume
    D: Simple Moving average
    E: Stochastic Ocs.
    F: Quote panel or Quote bar that streams the current information. Consider these study lines / bars as visual aids. If you learn some general chart activity using these parameters you'll see what your stock is doing on a daily basis and soon be able to see that the lines and bars are quite useful to you. It is better to have these visible indicators although you may not initially understand the information they convey. You will eventually develop "Charting Skills" that support your trading decisions. Charting is a valuable area of study to pursue but it will not be covered here because of the technical aspects are beyond the purpose of this composition.

4. Set up the stock scanning program that will help you find investment stocks that fit your criteria. It is not practical to start training with more than ten active stocks so the Top 10 on Monday will not be the top ten on Tuesday, you will be moved towards a variety on sector performance quickly using this simple method of picking your first stocks. You can listen to News that endorses stocks to buy or sell and act on them to get a feel of the accuracy in reporting (do not expect miracles). Buy reasonably and hold until your stop loss is activated or your sell trigger is activated. Keep in mind that the Soft Money (brokers fees) have to apply to all buys and sales transactions on stocks.

5.

6. Most stock scan programs have a nice list of top ten stocks to use when you first get started. Although the prices are spicy, you can start your practice in Paper-trading with these potentially hot stocks. If you do not have any set guidelines,

you can use these. The hottest selling stocks are normally good investments if you are a swing trader (in one day out the next) but the cost is so high they are dangerous because they have overkill on news that can drive prices quickly. The concern on this is that your preset exit may push you into Pattern Day Trader status quickly.

7. A stock scan for stocks with a Share Price = $2.00 to $39.00, Market Capitalization = $300 million to 2 Billion, P/E ratio = greater than 8 but less than 20, P/B Ratio = 2 to 7 or four, Net Profit Margin = greater than 10%, Free Cash Flow = greater than zero. By setting these parameters, you will bring up only stocks meeting these filters. Practice setting up filters, you may find stocks that fit your preferred filters.

8. Add at least one stock that has a high volume of Short Selling action and keep an eye on the activity. Compare speculative stock action with stable stocks.

9. Set your watch list, portfolio and charts to show pre-market and after hours trading. Ascertain whether you can trade NASDAQ / NYSE pre and after hours. After hours, trading is available to most traders.

10. When you set up your Paper-trading account, the brokerage will offer you a variety of start up cash accounts to choose from. Select the smallest monetary value as your account starting capital. Since most new investors in the real world start with only $5000.00 or less in real trading capital it is best to consider that you must try to stay within your real money account value even though you are in your Paper-trading account. With these limitations, you will quickly see how fast you can push yourself into dangerous margin situations and pattern day trading activities. A few transactions with these limitations will quickly show you how one can become insolvent even in a very good market. Although your limited account may still have value close to

the $5000.00, you can find yourself holding stocks that are all in negative cash territory that would be a loss if you sold them at this time. Getting all your capital tied up in negative value stocks moves you into the area of a spectator since you must sell a stock position and take a loss to get investment capital back into your account. When starting out in your Paper-trading account always sell your stock position when you have fifty dollars profit from the investment. You should have your Order Pre-Sets configured to do this.

CHAPTER 20
BUYING AMERICAN COMPANIES

Do not be fooled into thinking that you are buying an American Company stock. Hundreds of American Companies manufacture exclusively overseas / offshore etc.
In most sectors, you can search out the American companies and buy exclusively American Company stocks.
Checking out the fundamentals of the symbol, it will provide this information.
Reference: http://www.investopedia.com search the term fundamentals.
With the fast changing world market a great deal of stocks are traded on other World Exchanges. The opening and closing of the foreign exchanges can have an impact on your portfolio.
Changes in Foreign Currency can have devastating results if all your stocks are foreign companies.With over three dozen Chinese IPO's introduced into the American Stock Exchanges just this year (before August 1st. 2011) it is best to check out just where the Stock Originates from. (Find in fundamentals). They tend to trade substantially below their IPO prices very quickly. With 26 of the 2011 China IPO's trading below their IPO price, it is an important research point.

CHAPTER 21
REVERSE MERGERS

This is a new term for many investors. It is quite common in Chinese Companies and has happened several times this year in American Companies. In most situations, this is time to run from the stock or find your way out quickly.

Reference: http://www.investopedia.com search the term reverse mergers. http://www.flexfinancialgroup.com/reversemerger.html

CHAPTER 22
WEB BASED STOCK TIP SERVICES

Although there are hundreds of stock tip sheets and services on the Internet, you cannot depend on these freebie services to guide your stock purchases.

If you are going to sit at home and track every stock you own on a daily basis you could use some of the information offered to quickly enter and exit many of the trades that are suggested. However, this practice leads into day-trading and very risky transactions.

Practicing some of the trades in Paper-trading programs will give you a feel of what value the free information may cost you or profit you.

It is important that you maintain a notebook itemizing the trades you get from sources that you have not researched yourself. I use an EXCEL work sheet for this.

When you start exploring web based tip sheets and analyst reports I would suggest that you use your additional E-mail box at one of the free E-mail services. Always use this secondary box if you are required to log in or join for a 30-day free trial of the services offered. Even if you unsubscribe from the trial or tip sheet service you will still be getting E-mail from whomever they sell your Name and E-mail address to for an infinite period.

You can sign up for the credible Free News Letters at http://join.investopedia.com/investopedia/standard/step-1#axzz1Y1rpkV5F

Send these newsletters to your secondary mailbox.

You will start getting offers for financial tip sheets, free training seminars, free penny trading tip sheets just as soon as you get your first Paper-trading Account set up.

OTC/BB stocks change on a daily basis (American Companies) Stocks traded in OTC markets such as the OTCBB or Pink Sheets are usually thinly traded microcap or penny stocks, and both retail and institutional investors generally avoid them, because of fears that share prices are easily manipulated and there exists a potential for fraud.

The burden of the volume of the marketing mail you will be getting from brokers, tip sheets etc. is often overwhelming and can be disruptive to important communication you will be using in your primary email address.

Use this secondary box for registering on social media sites.

CHAPTER 23
SOCIAL MEDIA REPORTS

There is a high probability that any stock tip from Social Media sites is questionable.

News from social media is not news; it is the opinion of someone holding the stock and simply wants to enhance their position in the stock.

Reputable market reporting organizations avoid posting to questionable sites. This is especially true with penny stocks, over the counter stocks and bulletin board stocks that are very susceptible to pump and dump schemes.

After you open your trading account it will take only a few weeks before your name is harvested by many "Pump and Dump" entrepreneurs that will be sending you Email opportunities to get rich overnight buying their current project.

Anyone promising you very high profits on Bulletin Board, Pink-sheets and many OTC's could be attempting to start a momentum for a pump and dump maneuver.

You can see an example of this by searching on highest daily volume on stocks under $2.00.

> Many times linked sites from social media are harvesting your E-mail address so you can expect to get a few more fantastic offers each time you follow one of the links. Your secondary Email box will start filling before dawn each morning.

This is not a bad thing, you need to be informed and experience some of the fast action promised by these schemes. I would suggest that you Paper Trade some of the offerings to see for yourself the credibility of the information.

To get a real feel for trading Penny Stocks I suggest that you reset your Paper-trading program back to the original settings with no positions on any stocks.

From this point, take any or all of the stock tips you get through E-mail or other Penny Stock Tip sheets and buy about $100.00 of each stock. Try to keep the purchases in 100 stock lots so to simplify the quick math you will need to use evaluate your purchases.

Do not be surprised when your broker refuses to make transactions on stocks with a current value under $1.00

CHAPTER 24
BUYING EDUCATION

Mere minutes can make vast changes in the value of your stock portfolio.

In today's world of lightening fast Electronic Trading the trading is very efficient on all transactions. Along with the great improvement in executions on orders there are more "REAL" professional traders offering news, education, on line streaming educational events free.

While searching the Internet it is common to bring up old news stories, analyst reports and press releases when you search by the symbol letters. Pay attention to the date on the reports you are viewing and discard all but the very fresh information. News stories a week old is very long time in stock trading news, you need today's news.

Internet Search engines will have a link to free financial news normally under a clickable heading, FINANCE. A few of these are Yahoo, MSN, and Google.

Internet search engines do not all use the same news sources so you may need to visit several sites for the most current news by searching from several search engines.

There are many reputable sites for genuine news, but beware of Internet Entrepreneurs tip services that are not credible.

Brokerage trading software will have news links that you can trust and easily access from their trading page. Some of the news services provided free with your account and others are available through subscription.

Alternative news can be valuable and a quick search in your browser by stock symbol can bring in alternate news from other sources that are responsible reporters. Once your E-mail address is purchased by multiple brokerage firms you will start getting invitations to log onto Interactive Live Web Training Seminars. You will also receive invitations to attend Live Local seminars at local Hotels in your area.

Most of the local live seminars are free so you should get all the free education before you start buying expensive training.

When you attend one of the free full day seminars, you can expect a few hours of good quality education and then a few hours of a sales presentation before returning to the meat of the seminar.

If you are going to expand your knowledge of the stock market, by purchasing books on investments, remember to buy the most current books and research the most current information.

Buying books on stock trading is not discouraged but not absolutely required since almost everything you are buying in a recently published book is available free somewhere on the Internet. Once you are familiar with the basics of trading stocks will be good time to invest in an author that you have followed and respect.

When you purchase books be knowledgeable about the copyright and publication date. Some investment books can be considered timeless but considering our fast changing world I would suggest you stick with purchasing books published within the twenty-four month prior to the date you purchase.

CHAPTER 25
HOT LINKS

As you progress through the Paper-trading educational area you will need to start accumulation hot links (Favorites) that quickly bring up quality information related to the stock you are following.

1. News Feeds

2. Short Sale Interest

3. Ex Dividend Date

4. Date for quarterly reporting.

5. NASDAQ \ pre and after hours trading.

Much of this information is easily accessible through the trading software program you will be using in Paper-trading mode.

Your computer proficiency will be tested as you try to execute on the fly market research to support your stock portfolio activities. Keep a scratch pad handy, you will want to makes notes that you can refer to on a moment-to-moment basis as you perform research.

As you find interesting sites on investing start keeping them in your Favorites folder in your browser.

Keep a scratch pad handy, you will want to makes notes that you can refer to on a moment-to-moment basis as you perform research.

As you find interesting sites on investing start keeping them in your Favorites folder in your browser.

CHAPTER 26
STOCK PRICE MANIPULATION

With several hundred major trading firms it is NOT, uncommon for price manipulation to be active almost every day on a stock that one firm or many collaborate on the manipulation.

Denial of these charges is always the response of the perpetrating brokerages.

Take an example of Green Mountain Coffee, with brokerage X short selling 25,000 shares at $100.00 making the price move up. Brokerage B sells 30,000 shares at $98.00 quickly afterward allowing brokerage X to take in $2.00 per share within minutes or $50,000.00 in profits. Brokerage B has effectively lowered the current bid price to $98.00, which will continue a downward trend, and Brokerage B buys back in at $96.00 giving them $2.00 per shae or $60,000.00 in profits.

Do not kid yourself .... There are people of low morals and practically nonexistent ethics mixed in with the quality responsible traders. This happens almost every day. Remember the boys on Wall Street all drink in the same bars, use the same cocaine dealers, and share the same prostitutes, golf at the same clubs and vacation in the same resorts.

CHAPTER 27
A TOPIC ON OPTIONS, EVEN IF YOU ARE NOT TRADING OPTIONS

Giving the do not exercise instruction on an option is not necessary unless it finishes in the money. Options finishing out of the money expire automatically without any value and you need to do nothing.

Never enter the do not exercise instruction during the trading hours on the closing day on your options. If you want to issue the order for DO NOT exercise, enter the instruction after the trading day ends on Friday. Options actually close on Saturday and it will take until Monday for the instruction to become effective in your account balance sheet.

The do not exercise effectively closes your option position with you loosing the current market value. If you have an IN THE MONEY OPTION, always try to sell your option before market close.

CHAPTER 28
BUYING IPO'S

In the trading year 2011.

IPOs for the 2011 year finished lower within 48 hours than the IPO introduction price 63% of the time as of August 18.

With some experience watching Hot IPO introductions, you will get a feel for the proper timing for entry. However, Paper-trading these IPOs on open is great entertainment.

Chinese IPOs are notorious for fast losses. Be certain that your IPO is not one of the Chinese Reverser mergers that merge an unqualified Chinese company into a failing Chinese company for a quick listing on the American Exchanges. These reverse mergers often finish down considerably within a few days of entry and often just disappear as they are delisted when the value goes below $1.00 per share.

Do your researches before you buy IPOs?

Visit MSN-Money and check out IPO performance to get a good view of first day open and close scenarios.

Compare those opening prices to the current price to get a clearer picture of potentials.

END

ABOUT THE AUTHOR

Stan Wilder was born in Dallas Texas in the golden era right near the close of World War II.

After the perfunctory education, he traveled the world compliments of the US Navy.

Captured with the corporate dream he worked for Borg Warner, Purex, Diversy Corp. ,American Brands, Mizzy Dental before he started one of several entrepreneurial businesses related to computer Software Sales and Support.

Most recently, for the last six years he is involved in Real Estate Investments and Stock Trading on a full time basis.